BROKEN PIECES

A Mosaic of the Heart

Linnette L. Hayden

Broken Pieces a Mosaic of the Heart
Published by Total Fusion Press
6475 Cherry Run Rd. Strasburg, OH 44680
www.totalfusionpress.com

ISBN-10: 0988370085
ISBN-13: 978-0-9883700-8-1

Library of Congress Control Number: 2014937719

Cover Design by Linnette L. Hayden

Published in Association with Total Fusion Ministries, Strasburg, OH.
www.totalfusionministries.org

This book is dedicated to my family...

Family is far more to me than the people who share my bloodline. Family is about the people in my life that I have learned from, laughed and cried with, prayed over, encouraged, fought and made up with. We are completely imperfect people sharing life together and always being there for each other. There are even people that I am no longer in touch with that belong in this dedication because they had an impact on making me who I am and were part of my journey.

They are the people who love me enough to tell me the truth even when I don't want to hear it and even knowing I may make them miserable in the process. These people have shaped my life and were used by God to bring me to Him. I dedicate this book to my family of loved ones without whom my story would be much different, and to Linnea, my joy, my daughter, my life.

In addition, I want to thank my brother Darrell and my Sister-in-law Barb for giving me a home while I finished high-school. I was a mess but I was able to get a diploma and stay off the streets and that more than likely saved my life. I can't imagine too many young couples that would have wanted that kind of responsibility, but that's the kind of guy my brother is. I love you Darrell and I am eternally grateful to you both. By the way I'm still sorry about the wild party I had while you were gone. ☺ (Oh yea, and for ruining your beautiful Cougar XR7)

PREFACE

This is a story of a life so broken, and damaged that there was no hope for happiness, joy or even a reason to live. That is only the beginning of the story; joy, peace, and abundant blessing are the makings of the rest of the story. A life lived in freedom and purpose, dedicated to the savior that laid down His life for hers.

With an open mind and heart, grab a cup of tea and get ready to witness a transformation from darkness to light, fear to courage and loss to abundant gain.

In the beginning...

It would be impossible to tell this story without starting at the point when the earth moved, the known became unknown, and all that was trusted was lost...

THE NIGHT HER LIFE CHANGED FOREVER

It was in the wee hours of a cold January evening in 1969 when she woke up to hushed voices in the other room. As she struggled to focus and comprehend what she was hearing she suddenly heard a blood curdling scream that shook her to her very core. As she struggled to understand what she was hearing she recognized her grandmother's voice saying "no…no…no" then came a bloodcurdling scream that struck terror in her heart.

Her grandmother's screams had turned into whaling and uncontrollable sobbing. As she moved fearfully and carefully from the protection of the covers and out of bed she made her way into the living room. She saw two men that were very familiar to her; two of her parents friends and deacons of their church. Her grandmother had collapsed into the arms of one of the men and was practically in the fetal position while her grandfather sat in his chair completely silent and motionless.

A cold chill ran the entire length of her body as she stood frozen in the hallway trying to take in the scene that was playing out in front of her. One of the men came to her and put his arm around her shoulders and led her to the couch. As her legs moved and propelled her across the room in a robotic fashion she began to demand answers as to what was going on. As the answers began to come the words seemed to fall short of her ears as she began to drift in to a deep fog of confusion…her parents killed…car accident on the way home from her aunt and uncles…killed instantly…didn't suffer…she would be taken care of…What? None of this makes any sense! What are they talking about? Her parents won't come to get her in the morning? She would never see her father, her best friend ever again? She has to see her mom again, they argued on the way to grandmas and she said things she didn't mean, she had to tell her mom she was sorry!

She slipped into a muddy fog and although things were being said around her, about her and to her, she was not engaged in reality.
Numbness set in, she couldn't speak, or hear or move. It had to be a dream, no, a nightmare, so she would just go back to bed and she would wake up in the morning, Mom and Dad would be there to get her and everything would be just like they had planned. She went back to bed at her grandfather's cold and angry insistence and she decided that if she could go to sleep there was a good chance she would wake up and find this all to have been a horrible nightmare. She would wake up the next day and she wouldn't be abandoned, she wouldn't be an orphan and she would tell her Mom how sorry she was. She would tell both of them how much she loved them and they would hold her and tell her how much they loved her and the day would be just like any other day.

She woke up on January 30th with the realization that her life would never be the same…

A TWELVE YEAR OLD'S HEART

Abandoned, rejected, lonely, fearful, brokenhearted, betrayed: how could this loving God that she had heard about every day of her life take away the only two people she ever trusted? If this is what God's love is about, she didn't want anything to do with it! How could her parents leave her? Didn't they love her enough to stay? Her Dad had always promised to be there for her, he lied!

Her brothers didn't even seem to be upset. Her brothers were asking her questions about things in the house and what she wanted to do about tombstones and funerals and where she was going to live...all of this was madness! Why is this happening? All of this is wrong! They can't be getting rid of Mom and Dad's things; they can't sell the house that Dad built all by himself, why are they doing this? This can't be happening!

Does her reasoning make sense? Did her parents choose to leave her? Did God stop loving her because He took her parents? Was He punishing her for being a bad girl? Of course not! Were her brothers unmoved by all of this? Absolutely not! Her brothers were 6 and 8 years older than she was and already in college. They were taking care of what needed to be done and trying to include her in all the decisions. Could she recognize that at her age and in her confused and frightened state of mind? Were any of her thoughts mature and rational? How could they be? She was a twelve year old preteen who just suffered a trauma that would devastate any grown adult. Reason and logic has no place in a traumatized 12 year olds heart and mind.

Everyone complimented her on how well she did at the funeral. She never cried, she just quietly got through the day. The First Baptist Church was packed with standing room only as hundreds of people mourned Chuck and Doris Hayden. Two people they loved and who had made an impact on their lives. The front of the church was literally full of flowers but the most predominate fragrance was the smell of red roses; one of her mom's favorites. As soon as the doors opened for her to enter the church that day the smell of the roses seemed to overtake her senses and for a moment she thought she would choke.

A numb robotic young woman sat motionless in the 'family pew' for the double service as the Pastor honored her parents, and she stood in receiving lines and heard people talk about her parents as if they were saints. Her father was beloved by so many because of his award winning smile, and loving character. He was also very funny and enjoyed making people happy. Her mom was the perfect hostess. She was a great cook and no matter when you dropped by the coffee pot was on and within minutes there would be something to eat. As people filed through and shared their thoughts and memories, it started to become like white noise as she felt herself slipping into a world of her own to block out the pain as she would continue to do for the next 50 years. At the gravesite there was a moment when she fought back the urge to scream, because all she wanted was to be buried with them.

How do I know how she felt? That girl was me…

…and I still have a hard time with the smell of red roses…

LIFE AFTER DEATH

The death of my parents was the most life altering experience I had ever encountered at my young age. I was a bullied child at school from day one of kindergarten because I was fat, I wore glasses and now I even had braces! My home was the only place I didn't feel like a freak, except of course for when my brothers were around but what little sister doesn't, right?

My dad loved me unconditionally and he was my very best friend. I was close to my mom but it hadn't always been that way. My dad had a massive coronary the year before the accident and I watched my mom struggle through the month of his hospital stay. I heard her cry in her room every night pleading with the Lord not to take him before her because she couldn't live without him. I began to reach out to her because I realized this was something we had in common; we both loved and treasured my father.

One of the first clear thoughts I had after the accident was remembering those nights and thinking, "Mom's prayers were answered." Although that gave me comfort at times, there was a time I blamed her for her selfish request causing God to take them both. When something tragic happens there is always plenty of blame to go around. It is one of the ugliest stages of grief. There has to be someone to blame!

As the years went by, I blamed and blamed and blamed and ultimately the blame would always come back to me…I wasn't good enough or loveable enough for them to stay or for God to allow them stay with me. If I had been better they wouldn't have left.

11

I remember the first day I went back to school after the accident, one of the most notorious bullies in the school greeted me in his usual horrible way only this time he added a new twist to his 'you're so ugly..." heckling. This time it was, "You're so ugly your parents died from embarrassment!" I agreed.

At this point I had a court appointed guardian and they were good people. I knew them and liked them but trust wasn't something I had for anyone. The truth is it wouldn't have mattered where I was I wouldn't have been happy because it wasn't home. I was angry, and I had turned 13 that April so I was like any other typical teenager with raging hormones, more questions than answers and in my case...a desire to die.

I saw everything through the filter of anger, and mistrust. They were friends of my parents from church. They had one boy that my mom had watched when she was alive so I was used to him, but what I wasn't used to was the difference in how he was being raised and the way I had been raised. In my opinion he was spoiled rotten! They were wealthier than my parents and enjoyed spending their money on their son. Well, that is a natural thing to do but to a lonely outsider living on the 'inside' it felt like I was nothing in comparison.

It wasn't their fault, they did their very best but I wasn't their child and of course they would treat me differently. To a broken, scared and angry teenager, the differences were more fuel for anger and resentment. I began to resent them all, especially my foster brother. Even though I thought the woman was beautiful and I wanted to learn from her, I couldn't lay down my anger enough to really talk to her. The man was funny with a wonderful mix of common sense and practical wisdom. I never wanted him to know it but I listened and learned a great deal from him.

I put them to the test there is no doubt about that! They built a new house and even had a room for me in the plans and just when I thought things were starting to go as ok as they could be they told me it was too much for them and that I couldn't live with them anymore. Rejection, abandonment, worthlessness all over again! That was the defining moment when I knew that there was no place in this world for me, and that I would never be home again.

Anyone who said they cared about me was a liar! I would never trust anyone again! These people went to the same church I had grown up in and had been talking about the same God I had grown up hearing about and here we are…rejected once again. Thanks God, your hits just keep coming! Well I have had enough! You will not fool me again into believing that life will somehow be ok and that someone cares about me. You almost had me believing it but never again!

My oldest brother was married now so he and his wife took me in. We moved to a different city so I finished high school in a new town where no one knew my past or my situation. It helped but I also learned that people can be manipulated easily. I was so hungry for attention that I made up all kinds of lies to make people think I was someone special. Even negative attention was better than no attention at all. The problem with lies is they always catch up to you. When people no longer trust you they reject you.

As I look back I believe somewhere in my deepest pain I knew they would and that's why I did it. I couldn't trust that someone might actually care about me. I couldn't trust myself so I had to ruin everything so I could keep the anger hot and continue to fuel my self-destruction.

As time went by and I grew in to a young woman I lived in a make-believe world. I looked ok on the outside but on the inside I was losing touch with reality. I was so hungry for someone to care about me but so frightened of caring for someone that would leave me that I sought out anything that would numb the pain. I was so insecure that even when people did reach out to me I didn't trust them and I drove them away with my manic behavior.

Psychologists, psychiatrists, clergy, you name it; they all tried to 'figure me out'. I had become such a good liar that I could even manipulate the professionals. The 'medical' professionals always wanted to give me drugs to "stabilize my moods." Well, that was great for me because the more numb I could be the better. I began to go from doctor to doctor. Since I knew what they wanted to hear to get a prescription out of them, I was never without drugs. I put on such a 'goodie-two-shoes' act that no one suspected a thing. All those years in church had paid off now because I knew how to talk and carry off that look to a tee.

Drugs quickly led me to self-medicate with alcohol, then marijuana, and the biggie, sex. As much as I could get them as often as I could get them! Sex was a huge drug for me! It gave me those few moments of someone's arms around me and that feeling of being connected but I didn't have to care about them or wonder if they cared about me. I just wanted those few moments of make-believe and then I could be numb again.

As I continued to suppress the sting of rejection and abandonment I began to harden my heart to people completely. I put on a great show, the party girl with the quick wit and the devil may care attitude. Reality however set in as each sexual encounter ended, or the hang over reminded me I could feel something, and the scared lonely 12 year old would resurface, I was back to blaming myself and God for every ugly breath I took. I was unworthy of love, I was unworthy of any good thing, and now I was too damaged and broken to ever be of any use to anyone or myself again.

A NEW LIFE BEGINS

12 years after the death of my parents, God began to lay out His plan to bring me back...he gave me a child. At 25 I gave birth to a beautiful baby girl and I had never been more terrified of anything in my life! How was I going to take care of this little life? How was I going to care for her when I couldn't even take care of myself? How could I feel anything for her when I couldn't feel anything for myself or anyone else? For the last ten years or more I spent most of everyday praying that something would kill me and make the pain stop for good. Now I was responsible for another human being! How could I reconcile the two; loathing myself and what I had made of my life, but needing to care for someone else and make a life for them when all I could feel was pain and anger and worthlessness?

God in His infinite wisdom knew that once I began to feel love again, it would open the flood gates for me to begin to heal. I was by no means a good mother in the early years but each day I began to change and my heart began to soften. One day when my baby girl was 18 months old she hurt herself and I remember being overwhelmed with emotions. I realized that day that I would lay down my life to protect her, and as I felt the first real tears I had shed in a decade streaming down my face, I knew the healing had begun. The healing of my heart began to change how I saw myself, and the world around me. I knew that I had to make a better life for her than I was living and I knew I owed that to her.

Despite my anger with God, I knew Truth and I knew I wanted her to know it too. You see all the years that I was running from God, there was one thing I couldn't run away from and that was the knowledge I had of Truth. I was very angry with God but I never denied Him. I knew right from wrong and that is what fueled my run from Him, doing everything I could that I knew was wrong, because I wanted to hurt Him like He had hurt me!

The Truth still lived in me though. For example I couldn't stand to hear the Lord's name taken in vain. I swore like a mule-skinner but I would never disrespect His name. What this says is that all the training my parents and the church had given me was still there. I knew right from wrong and when I would hear the Lord's name in vain it would give me physical pain. That foundation of faith was still there and that is what the Father built His plan on to direct my path back to His loving arms. I wanted my daughter to have that in her life even though I was still mad at God I knew in my heart that the Bible was Truth. I believed it was too late for me, because of all the choices I had made, but it wasn't too late for my baby girl.

Of all the gifts my parents gave me, the knowledge of Jesus Christ was the most precious of them all. I will be eternally grateful (literally!☺) for their insistence that we were in church on Sunday, (and all the other times the church was open!) and that we read and understood our Bible and that we knew Jesus died on the cross to save us. We lived it out in our home and Mom & Dad set the example of Christ every day. Without that grounding in the Word, I know for a fact that I would be dead in a ditch somewhere, never knowing the fullness of Joy that I live in today.

Thank you Mom and Dad for loving me enough to teach me the Truth!

BROKEN PIECES

My life had become a junk heap of broken dreams, broken trust, abandonment, rejection filth and lies. The pieces of my life made me feel less than human, definitely less than a woman, and not even close to whole enough to be a mom.

Brokenness is tiring. You spend most of your time trying to keep your pieces together while at the same time trying to hide them from the world. You are a captive of your own making. You are trapped in a game of the enemies making and he makes up the rules to suit himself. Whenever you try to climb out he has another lie to knock you back down.

I hid behind a quick wit and a dazzling smile but inside I was screaming in pain and anger. As soon as someone started to try and get close to me I would do something horrible to push them away. I was always protecting myself from the next hurt. However, there were times I would latch onto someone so hard that I smothered them and I would play mean mind games to "test" their devotion to me, until they couldn't take it any longer and they would flee. Either I refused to see what I was doing or in reality I probably didn't even know but what I did know was that love was not an option for me.

REJECTION

Rejection is one of the major contributors to the broken pieces of my life and has shaped me through most of my first 50 years and it even reared its ugly head again when I moved to Ohio. Rejection is something that can manifest itself in many ways. It can make you fearful to try new things; it can keep you from participating in activities where you may be judged on your performance. It will make you push people away, and it will cause you to judge others harshly before they can judge you first because you know they will.

I was a bartender for many years and I always ran a lively bar. My quick wit and my sharp tongue made for many nights of slicing and dicing people all in the name of good clean bar fun. That was an outlet for me to put all that anger and hurt into a neat little package called 'the joke'. As I continued to deliver my jokes people laughed and enjoyed the wit and 'one-upmanship' that I was so good at. I was so good that I could cut someone off at the knees and they would laughingly come back for more. I look back on those days now and realize that all those people were as broken as I was and I now I know I was responsible for speaking words of death over them and myself at the same time.

The words that are spoken to us and over us and about us affect us in greater ways than almost any other influence. Our words have the power of life and death in them and when all you can feel is death, then that is all you speak. Rejection breeds rejection, and that is the enemies reoccurring theme with all of his ugly tools…he sucks you in with his lies (rejection, abandonment, etc.) and one lie breeds another lie and another until you are so broken and beaten down from all the falsehoods you have come to believe that the lie is now your view of reality.

Reality is far from what the enemy wants us to believe about rejection. The reality is that Christ never rejects us. He went to the cross to give us a blood covering that hides our sin from the Father. He covers us and He is always there with open arms when we run to Him. Rejection isn't in His character. Ask yourself this, "Why would He have suffered on the cross to reject us now?" If sin was going to keep Him from loving us then the cross would have been a worthless act. When I finally started to understand that it didn't even matter if people rejected me because Jesus never does, it opened a whole new world for me, actually it was a whole new Kingdom! ☺

I am a lover of words and I found it interesting when I looked up the word reject(ion) in Webster's, one of the definitions started with to "spew out...". Well nowhere in the Bible does it talk about Jesus spewing out anything as He spoke, however that is exactly the language used in describing the communication skills of the enemy. If someone is spewing words of rejection or any type of hurtful or demeaning words, that is straight from the pit of hell and you need to run to the open arms of Jesus and the Word of hope, light and Truth.

The only acceptance of any true value is the acceptance of your place in the kingdom and the understanding that you will never be rejected by the King. You are His precious child for whom He has abundant love and eternal blessings!

"Every time I thought I was being rejected from something good I was actually being redirected to something better." - Steve Maraboli

ABANDONMENT

Another contributing factor to my brokenness was abandonment. Losing Mom & Dad affected me far greater than I ever understood and it was because of the deep sense of abandonment. I can honestly say that it wasn't until just recently at 57 years old that I finally feel 'at home'. I have lived with a feeling of 'waiting until....happens and then I'll...' for as long as I can remember. I never felt like I belonged anywhere so where I was never felt like where I was supposed to be, so I was always waiting for the next thing.

The pure definition of abandonment means to leave someone without protection or support. Well, trust me when I tell you that a 12 year old girl without her parents feels pretty unprotected and without support. We are naturally drawn to people who support us and protect us and that gives us comfort. Comfort is something I never knew after Mom and Dad were gone. I think that was what I missed the most. Knowing someone cared and would help me if I needed it. They weren't being paid to take me in or helping me out of some sense of duty but they really truly cared about me.

Abandonment played itself out in my life in several ways. One of them is being a packrat! I can't throw anything away! Stop! Don't call Hoarders, I'm working on it! ☺ I have come a very long way in that area but it still cause's me physical pain to throw away certain things.

When I moved to Ohio I took huge steps in getting rid of things, especially things that had been given to me by family members. Up to this point I couldn't let anything go that had anything to do with family. They took on almost shrine-like status in my mind until I recognized that it was a compulsion driven by the need for family and trying to feel like I had someone around me that cared. When it came time to move I knew I had to part with some things. I was actually able to part with a lot of things and when it came to stuff from the relatives, that was tough, but it was really easy when it was a relative I didn't even like and I knew they wouldn't be coming to Ohio to see if I was using it! ☺

Abandonment also kept me isolated. Isolating myself from any real emotion for anyone because I always knew they would leave. After my daughter was born the isolation became even greater because now I had to make sure no one hurt her either! The big problem with that was in isolating myself I isolated her and she never really had a chance to learn how to be open with people. She became very guarded and untrusting too. So in my attempt to protect her, I harmed her in many ways. You see when we are hurting we hurt the people around us and it is usually the people that are the most important to us.

The good news about abandonment is that the character of Christ is about being a Rock, stable strong and never moving. Jesus isn't going anywhere! Even in those times when He feels far from us, it is never Jesus that moves! He promises to never leave us or forsake us! He is always there to count on for protection, support and comfort. This has been very hard for me to come to grips with because I blamed God for the abandonment of my parents so I couldn't trust that He would never leave me because in my mind He already did.

The important thing to remember in all things is that God knows our heart. Even when our actions are sinful and our behavior is manic God is looking at our heart. He has always known how I felt about Him and He has always known why I did the things I did. Through it all He looked at my heart and in His loving and patient way, drew me back to Him. You see He didn't go anywhere the whole time I was running as hard and as fast as I could, He never moved. Abandonment is not in His character, He is not capable of abandoning His children.

WORTHLESSNESS

My self-image was so low that I not only felt I was worthless but I was certain that everyone else knew I was worthless too. Everything that was said to me I heard through the filter that said "they think you are stupid/ugly/worthless etc." so I reacted as if that was exactly what they said instead of just honestly listening. I anticipated the worst and couldn't see anything different even when it wasn't there. It kept me from trying new things because I was sure I couldn't do it well enough and then when I did give something a try I made myself sick obsessing over it until it was perfect. Then if I didn't get the reaction I thought I should have received for my outstanding effort then I threw myself back into the depths of shame and worthlessness and told myself I was stupid to even try. Most of the time my efforts were accepted well but I wasn't hearing what was said, I was hearing through the filter and only heard the worst.

The enemy is that filter that causes us to believe the lies because he is the prince of liars! The farther down he can keep us the more control he has over us. What better way to turn you away from the Creator than to hate the creation?

God's message to you about your worth couldn't be more different! He made you with a purpose in mind, a specific purpose for you! How NOT worthless can you be! The secret to overcoming the desperation of worthlessness is to seek His purpose for your life. He takes everything in our life, all the broken pieces, the good the bad and even the very ugly and remakes it into something beautiful, useful and of great value.

I still struggle in this area especially in the area of my weight. I was born 10lbs and I have been heavy ever since. I have always had a problem with my weight. The only time I was thin was when I was hyped up on speed and living on coffee, cigarettes and alcohol. It was amazing to me how people treated me so differently when I was thin and 'beautiful'. I had never been more troubled and screwed up than when I was 'attractive' but that was the only time people treated me as if I had value. Trust me when I tell you that what you 'see' in people with your eyes is rarely who they really are. You have to see people with your heart, and the eyes of Christ.

Although this is the area that has taken me the longest to understand and to turn around, and I am still working on it every day, I know now that I am not worthless. I know this because God has shown me His love for me unconditionally. I choose to focus on today and the purpose for the day, not on my past. I focus on God, His purpose for me and my gratitude for all He provides. Look to the heart of people even when it is the most difficult. Remember, hurting people hurt people. The love of Christ heals.

PRICKLY = IT ISN'T JUST ABOUT CACTUS

Have you ever cared for someone that was so sensitive that you had to weigh every word you said and every glance you made in fear of offending them until you just began to avoid being around them because it took so much work? Well, hello...that was me for over 50 years! I was so consumed with being inadequate I couldn't trust that anyone else saw me any differently. The brokenness of bad choices and a reckless lifestyle had kept me trapped inside with all my ugliness reminding me every minute that I was worthless. The choices I had made kept me in a constant state of self-loathing and self-hatred, so how could anyone else think anything good about me? If they knew everything I had done, they would hate me too.

Not long ago, someone whom I love very much and who has seen the Lord change my heart over time used the word 'prickly' to describe what I used to be like. That really stuck with me and I began to think about what it means to be prickly. When you think of a cactus, is your first thought to run up and give it a hug? Yea, well if it is you may have some serious issues of your own! ☺ Anyway, no, of course not, your first thought is stand back and proceed with caution!

That's what it is like to try and care for someone who is so sensitive that they make it uncomfortable to be around them. As I look back on the many years that I was in a loving church who supported me and provided for me and showed me in abundant ways that they truly cared for me and loved me with the love of Christ, I realize what I must have put them through. I got to the point that if I heard the words,

"You are so sensitive" or "Don't be so sensitive" one more time I was going to show them how insensitive I could really be! When you are living in a self-hell of your own making, you can't see anything from someone else's point of view. Self-loathing and self-hatred is the greatest form of selfishness there is! The whole world revolves on your axis and as you continue to spin the view never changes and it is never pretty!

I was a Youth leader in my church, I had turned my life over to the Lord and was truly seeking Him in all things. I was writing wonderful curriculum for Sunday School, and VBS and had started a Saturday morning program for the neighborhood kids as well as going on mission trips and winning people to Christ on a regular basis but I was as prickly as they come! No matter how much I 'did for the Lord', or how much praise I received from people, deep down inside I still felt worthless and unlovable.

If you think of a cactus, they have some of the most beautiful flowers in their season, but you can't get to the flower because the needles are too sharp. That's what happens when we are so focused on ourselves, we may be producing beautiful things but our true beauty goes without full appreciation because no one is allowed close enough to see it.

There was one person in that time who saw the core of me and loved me enough to tell me the truth, and for that I am eternally grateful. Pastor Paul Strahan, of Des Moines Fellowship church started me down the path of learning to love and forgive myself. Pastor Paul is truly the closest person to Christ like of anyone I have ever known. He always speaks the truth in love and doesn't shy away from saying what the Lord has put on his heart even when he knows the person may have trouble hearing it. He cares enough about people, and is obedient to the Lord when he is called upon to say and do what needs to be said and done. I moved from Des Moines before I made significant improvement in the prickly department but I am praying that one day, I will be able to deliver the flower from the cactus to him and say thank you for starting me on the path to telling myself the truth and becoming 'prickly free'.

DE-PRICKLING ☺

Why do cacti have needles? Protection & defense! Why do we get prickly? Protection & defense! Why do we feel the need to be protected? What are we defending ourselves from? What are we afraid of? Is the danger real or is it simply our perception? There is a big difference in fearing that a gunman holding a gun to your head may actually shoot you than the fear of someone saying something that will hurt your feelings or make you feel bad, but isn't the latter more often the case? (If not, you should probably hangout in different places! ☺)

Learning to start being less reactive to people starts with understanding who we are. First of all we are fearfully and wonderfully made by a God who has a purpose for our lives. He made you the way you are and has brought you to and through the things in your life to prepare you for His ordained purpose. To see yourself as less than a beautiful creation of the living God says that you think God's creations are inferior.

We are all imperfect people loved and created by a perfect God. In our weakness He reveals His strength. It isn't until we see ourselves as totally dependent on Him that we can then understand our importance. Does that make sense? Well, in the worldly view of importance no, because we are told to be strong and capable, never show fear, be independent, a free thinker, overachiever etc. So if we are totally dependent on someone else how can we be of any personal importance or value? Because when we fully understand the value He has placed on us we realize that what we do and say impacts the kingdom as a whole!

We are created for a specific purpose so in carrying out that purpose we are kingdom changers! He enables us to do more than we can ever hope or imagine. How good does it feel when your boss chooses you for a special project at work? Makes you feel good to be recognized doesn't it? Well God has chosen you for a purpose that will have a far greater impact than any power point presentation or any profit and loss statement.

We have been called by God Himself to carry out a purpose of eternal importance! When He calls us He provides every resource needed. What He calls you to, He will see you through. We weren't created to be perfect without Him; we were created to be perfected in Him. You couldn't possibly be more important!

The more we focus on ourselves the less focus we have on God. When we are focused on ourselves we see all that we can't do but when our focus is on God, we see that nothing is impossible! We have to see ourselves through His eyes and not our own. Yes we have all done things we are not proud of and yes it is hard to see past failures and insecurities but when we become Christians we start fresh! We are born again completely, meaning the old life is gone and we are now completely new! We are working under a whole new authority and we have a fresh start with a new beginning.

When we hold our past against ourselves or allow what people say and do to affect how we see ourselves, we have stopped seeing ourselves through the eyes of the Lord. Nothing can be seen more clearly than when it is seen through the eyes of its creator. It doesn't matter what it is, when someone creates something, they know what will make it perform at its best, what it needs to work safely and when it needs maintenance or support. That is how God sees us. People will always find fault in other people but God doesn't look for fault, He is busy working all things together for your good, because you are made for His purpose. The bible doesn't say He only works out the good stuff you do, it says He works ALL things together for good. (Romans 8:28)

When you seek God's approval and live to be in His will, the approval of others becomes a non-issue. We die to ourselves when we become new creatures so just think, you can't offend a dead person! Basque in His love and acceptance and your joy will overflow.

Needles should be reserved for sewing, cactus and Christmas trees, but not for people! ☺

BECOMING A NEW CREATION

We have all heard the analogy of salvation explained as a caterpillar changing into the new life of a butterfly, and although it is a beautiful picture, how does it really happen for us.

First we have to understand the nature of the caterpillar which represents each of us without Christ. Caterpillars are simply the larvae of a butterfly; the early stage of a more beautiful creation. All caterpillars were created to become a butterfly. We are all created to be a new creation in Christ. Not one caterpillar was created to stay a caterpillar. Do they all make it without getting squished? No, but no matter what, if they live they are designed to become a butterfly. Do all of us make it to salvation? No, but we are all designed to come to the Father and become new. God gave us a will to choose because He wants us to come to Him freely and with a heart after Him.

The caterpillar has one focus and that is to seek out food and devour it. Farmers and gardeners regard caterpillars as pests because of all the damage that they do to the plants and crops. As people without the Lord, we are self-centered and seek only what pleasures us, and often leave destruction in our wake. That's why so many people are in a state of hopelessness because all they can see around them is the debris of a life lived without purpose while solely focused on themselves and their own agendas.

Butterflies on the other hand are welcomed in to fields and gardens not only for their beauty but they provide a valuable service by helping to propagate the plant life. Some gardeners plant whole gardens dedicated to attracting butterflies. We have all heard of 'Butterfly Gardens' but have you ever heard of a 'Caterpillar Garden'?

We as God's people should be welcomed and we should be providing a service to all those around us. We have a job to be propagating and helping others grow too, just like the butterfly. When the caterpillar becomes a butterfly he no longer crawls along the ground, he starts to rack up frequent flier miles to all the best gardens in the area!

When the caterpillar creates the cocoon it takes all the junk from his caterpillar life with him. All the pain he has endured, all the wrong turns he's made, all the crud he's crawled through is all in there with him. Yet when the butterfly emerges as a new creation, the whole creature has changed. Although the butterfly has 'a past' as a creeping crawling caterpillar, the new life of the butterfly has taken on a whole new character. There is no resemblance from the old to the new. While the old held it down and kept it working so hard to move very far very slowly, the new creation is free to fly and free to really live bringing joy and beauty wherever it goes.

The change doesn't come easy but it is worth it! If you have ever seen a butterfly preparing to escape the cocoon, you know that there is a lot of work involved. I read a story one time about a man that happened upon a cocoon and he was fascinated to see the butterfly working out its escape. He felt so sorry for the butterfly because it was writhing and twisting and pushing and on and on, so he decided to help it along. As soon as the butterfly had freed itself the man realized he had made a mistake. The butterfly was weak and unable to use its wings properly. You see the work involved in freeing itself from the cocoon was necessary to make the butterfly strong enough for the flight ahead.

Many of us are in the cocoon stage. We are fighting our circumstances and kicking and screaming along the way, but the good news is that you can stop fighting now. You are a new creation so it's time to shed the cocoon and fly! That's it, kick off the remnants of that cocoon, shed the old life and fly!

We are selfish by nature but when we are changed into a new creature we take our eyes off of ourselves and we have the eyes of Christ. The eyes of Christ are merciful, full of grace and compassion. They are not self-seeking or rude. They hold no record of wrongs, and they seek peace. Sound familiar? That is the definition of love from Chapter 13 of Corinthians. Christ sees us with the eyes of love and that is how we should see others. When people hurt you and upset you, try this simple prayer that always helps me; "Father let me see them through your eyes and help me see them the way I pray you see me". It can save you from many hurt feelings and misunderstandings. You are a new creation with all new parts including your eyes, the eyes of grace. Grace for yourself and for others.

STARTING THE TRANSFORMATION

I know I have talked about myself and my journey, and I have told stories about butterflies and so forth but what does of any of this mean to you? I want you to know that even though you are feeling broken there is hope! There is no place so low that the Lord can't reach down and pull you up. He wants to do that! He really does! He is not like the people we know that say they will be there for us but then when we need them they are nowhere to be found. That is not in His nature!

He is the comforter, the counselor, the constant companion. I love that! You should see me when I am driving in my van; I talk to the Lord like He is sitting right next to me. It is actually pretty funny when we are in a deep conversation and someone pulls up at the stop light and I'm talking to the seat! HA! ☺ That is how His presence really is! You can talk to Him and He will talk back! No not audibly however that can happen as well but when you are in a personal relationship with Christ, you will hear His voice. How cool is that! The Son of God talks to me and He wants to communicate to you as well. Would you like that? Who wouldn't? Quite frankly if you don't then you are not ready to move past the condition you are in. The only way out of brokenness is healing and healing comes from the Great Physician, our Father in heaven.

Are you ready to get started? Let's go... ☺!

PUTTING THE PIECES TOGETHER

I am so glad you stayed with me because the transformation journey will change your life beyond anything you can imagine! You have to decide if you are ready to be sold out and committed to the purpose God has for you. If you are still reading then you are like me, you want everything God has to offer and you are willing to make whatever changes necessary! You see the only one who can take your brokenness and make it a beautiful mosaic is your Father in heaven. This is not Linnette's plan for success, this is God's plan for His people and it is outlined clearly in His Word.

Step One: Relinquish Complete Control
Yea I can hear you now..."oh no!" - "I have to stay in control" - "It is MY life after all!" - "I will have to give up too much!" "I will have to change too much" etc... Well, I have a question for you..."How's that working out for you so far?"

I really struggled in this area and the truth is that sometimes it still rears its ugly head. By nature I am a control freak. In event planning I was meticulous about every detail and I often found myself burned out and frustrated because I spent so much energy fixated on every little thing that I would make it difficult for people to work with me. They knew what I wanted, they were well trained but I hovered over them so much and often 'redid' their work to the point that I had really good people walk out on me.

One of the most important lessons I ever learned was the art of collaboration. Collaborating doesn't diminish your importance or your contribution; it in fact makes it stronger and more valuable because it is supported by the contributions of others. Controlling everything leaves you all alone to enjoy your successes and miserably alone to suffer your mistakes. Learning to relinquish control gives you great freedom!

I began to experience a great joy in helping people find their own creativity and giving them the freedom to express their gifts in their own way. There is wisdom in understanding that even though something wasn't done 'your way' it still got done and the world didn't come to an end! ☺

Because of my controlling nature learning to relinquish complete control to the Father has been the most difficult process of my life. So if you are thinking that you can't do it believe me I understand, but trust me when I tell you that you will never experience real joy, until you do.

Think about it for a second, do you know the future? Do you know the inner workings of your body…your mind? (actually the thought of knowing the inner workings of my mind scares me a little!) ☺ Do you know the future for anyone else? If you planned and schemed for a week, could you guarantee any outcome at any time? No of course not so why is it so hard to turn the controls over to the one who does know the future? He does know your mind, the mind of others, and more importantly He knows your heart, those inner desires and places that you don't even let yourself visit very often because they seem so impossible.

He created us and He knows every detail of our lives. He knows our future because He created us for a purpose and He is preparing us to walk that out. When I want to control a situation I want to know as many details as possible so I know what I may be up against. Well, in the game of life we have no idea what may be around the corner, but your Father in heaven does and He has gone before you to prepare the way. It is hard to argue that the one who knows all the variables and how to control them should be the one in charge.

The Creator is the only one that knows exactly how something is made and how it will perform at its best. God created you, every part of you and He made you for a specific purpose. He knows the parts you need and He knows what is required for your maintenance. For example, if someone was going to set out to build a lawnmower he would not use parts from a blender. Why not? They both have blades, right? They both have blades but they have different purposes. If the lawnmower breaks down will the owner take it to a toaster mechanic? No because a toaster mechanic doesn't have an expertise in lawnmowers!

That may seem like a silly example but it is really that simple. The purpose God has for me is different than the purpose He has for you but the fact that He is the Creator and knows each of us intimately, piece by piece ensures that He knows what is best for us. As I saw God's plan start to lie out before me I realized that many of the painful experiences I have had and the pain I have caused myself are all now being used for His honor and His glory. Without my past I would not have the understanding that I have for those in abusive relationships, for bullied children, or the fearful, abandoned, rejected and broken lives that God has blessed me to serve.

I don't have formal degrees and special education with doctorates and a bunch of letters after my name so in the eyes of the world I am not qualified to minister to people. The difference is that I may not be 'qualified', but I AM CALLED! God has called me to His purpose of sharing my story to help others. There is no greater calling than to be in His service for the purpose of building His Kingdom! There is nothing worthless about that!

I fought with God for decades because I was angry with Him for His choices in my life. Even though I ran from Him as fast and as hard as I could, He never left me and He never stopped loving me. I know this because as I look back, His hand was on me, protecting me and providing for me even in my brokenness.

Let go of the controls! He knows you better than you know yourself and He knows all your pieces and how to mold them together into your own beautiful mosaic.

APPLICATION:

Take a few minutes and think about what you need to give over to God. Pray for His wisdom and clarity. In what areas do you struggle with control? Write them down.

_____

_____

_____

_____

Now commit these areas to the Lord in prayer. There is power in writing things down and then praying over them. The Lord will reveal Himself in the process and you will find freedom as you begin to turn over the control.

Now take a minute and think about your responsibilities. All of them, family, work, church socially etc. List them below:

_____

_____

_____

_____

_____

_____

_____

_____

_____

_____

_____

_____

Now as you look at the list I want you to look at each area and ask yourself, "How much can I honestly control?" Write it down next to the item. If you are really honest there is very little that we have complete control over.

Ok, now the next question may be a little more painful; "why do I want control in that area?" Now is when you need to get really honest with yourself because most of the time our desire for control has selfish motives. Ouch, I know, sorry but I promised to always speak Truth so there it is. I am speaking from experience here. I didn't go to Control Freak 101 classes I am just sharing with you what the Lord has shown me through years of brokenness and pain and ways that I brought it on myself. You may want to make some notes here because these notes you are making is a way to direct your prayer life and it is also a journal. You can come back and see how far you've come from this point when you gain freedom in these areas.

_____

_____

_____

_____

Now look at the list and ask yourself how many of these responsibilities should you really have. Are you taking on more than you should? Look back at the last question and see if your motives are directing you to take responsibility for something simply so you can control the outcome. If so, the responsibility more than likely belongs to someone else.
Perfectionism will also cause us to take control that doesn't belong to us. "I might as well do it myself so I know it gets done right." Sound familiar? Learning to trust that sometimes things just need to be done, and

your way isn't always the only way can be one of the most freeing experiences ever!

I go through a checklist like this every day in my prayer time because I still have times when I apparently think I'm Superwoman and I take on more than I should. I ask Him to show me what is from Him and what shouldn't be on my plate that day. There is great freedom in learning to delegate and even better, learning to say NO! ☺ No really, I'm not kidding, it is a real word and you have permission to use it! ☺ God will direct your path and He will give you the strength and resources to accomplish everything He has called you to do. If you are overwhelmed and things aren't coming together in an area, it might be that it was never yours to handle in the first place. Relinquish control to the Father and experience the peace that comes from knowing you don't have to be all things to all people. God already has that job and He is the only one that can do it well.

STEP TWO: Tell yourself the Truth

So you must start by telling yourself the Truth! The words we use change the outcome of our lives. People speak death into their lives and the lives of those around them every day and don't even realize the damage they are doing. The Word is very clear that the power of life and death are in the tongue. So every time you speak you are making changes to the outcome for those who hear, and since every time you speak you hear it, your mouth is affecting you constantly. We will be looking at the power of our words extensively in Step Seven.

Ok, so we have to tell ourselves the Truth. What Truth is that you may ask? Well let's start with who you are. 1 Peter 1:9 tells us we are the Chosen People, a Royal Priesthood, and God's Own Possession. You are royalty; you are a child of the Living God and a member of the royal family. Stop! Don't look at your current surroundings and say, "Ha! These ramen noodles, past due bills and thrift store clothes do not add up to royal living!" Feeling a little far from the palace are we? Don't look at your circumstances look at the King! Your Daddy is the King!

If you aren't experiencing royal living then it is time for you to make your way to the palace! It starts with a mindset. Colossians 3 tells us to set our minds on things above and not on the things of this earth. We get so bogged down by our circumstances we forget to look at who is greater than our circumstances and the one who always has our best interest in mind. It starts with what we think about and what we say about who we are. Ok practice right now, are you ready?

Repeat after me...1, 2, 3...GO!

"I am a child of the King! I am fearfully and wonderfully made! I am covered in the Blood of the Lamb! I am the righteousness of Christ! My mouth is a vessel of praise! I am a member of the Royal Family! I am beautiful in the eyes of the Lord! I was made for a purpose in the Kingdom! I have a high calling! I wear grace and mercy! I am loved! I am Royalty! I walk in favor of the Most High God!"

Ok, now if that didn't make you smile a little or sit up straighter or even lift you up a little then you need to go back and say it over and over again until you start to feel something shifting in your soul. The Truth will change you from the inside out.

We need to start telling ourselves the truth of who we are and start walking in that Truth. If you were in a royal gown with a tiara and servants were at your beck and call, do you think you would carry yourself differently? At the very least the way we carried ourselves would distinguish us as royal. Head up, shoulders back confident and British...oops sorry, that was just me, lover of the British accent dreaming again! Ok so not British but you get the picture, the royal look.

When people see us they need to see the signs of our heritage, the confidence of our bloodline, the bloodline of Christ. That doesn't mean arrogance or a lording over attitude it simply means that we don't shake and crumble, we stand confident when things get tough. We know who we are and more importantly we know <u>whose</u> we are! People should see in us a pride in our lineage. Not because of who we are but because of who our Father is, the King!

You see that is true humility, when we know that who we are means nothing without knowing who it is we belong to. We are nothing without the Father but with Him we can do ALL things! When we are moving in His will the path is made straight for us to follow and He goes before us to clear the way. Tell yourself the Truth ... "I can do ALL things through Christ because He is my strength!"

No matter what the situation you are facing, His grace is sufficient and His mercy is there for you when you fail. He will never let you go and you can't go so far that He can't pick you up and carry you back to Him. I know this for a fact because I am living proof! HE LOVES YOU!!!! HE MADE YOU!!!! HE LOVES YOU JUST THE WAY YOU ARE! All the brokenness, all the doubts and fears make you who you are and He loves you so much that He is taking all those pieces and putting them together into a beautiful masterpiece. There it is, are you ready?

Repeat after me ...1, 2, 3...go! "I am a beautiful masterpiece in the hands of my Father!"
Rinse, repeat! Sorry, no rinsing just repeating!

Say it all the time! Especially in those moments when you aren't 'feeling it'...you know, like when you put the cereal in the refrigerator and the milk in the cabinet. What? Am I the only one? Anyway, remember that what you tell yourself becomes your reality. Words change the atmosphere once they are released so be careful what you are saying to yourself and the people around you.

APPLICATION:

Ok, it's that time again. Time to ask yourself some questions.
When you do something silly what do you say?
When your husband/child/wife/coworker does something wrong, what do you say? The first thing out of your mouth, what is it usually? Write them down.

_____

_____

_____

_____

Ok look at the words you speak, (you were honest right?) is there anything that could be damaging to you or to them? Something as simple as, "Really, did you really do that?" can make a person feel pretty stupid! How about, "I am such an idiot!" Yea, I struggle with that one! You are not an idiot you did something silly, that is not who you are! When you call yourself a name that enters your soul and the enemy feeds on that with more lies of insecurity and doubt. I have changed mine to "Yes I'm special and that's why I am Jesus's favorite project!" ☺

It's your turn, how can you take the things that come out of your mouth without thinking and change them in to something more encouraging? Practice a little here.

_____

_____

_____

STEP THREE: Approval from God Not Man

I am so encouraged by some of the big name organizations that have had to take a stand for their faith recently. Hobby Lobby is one that is a beacon of light in this dark and conforming world. They are willing to close their doors and lose millions before compromising their faith. I applaud them and what they are doing but what is disturbing is that they are one of a very, very few.

To stand up to the world seems to be more than most Christians want to take on for fear of criticism, rejection or the most disturbing of all, apathy. The world should recognize us as children of the King, the Royalty of our generation, we should be set apart. It isn't a confrontational stand it is simply an uncompromising one. What we do and say on this earth has eternal rewards, and/or consequences. There is no half way so taking an apathetic approach will never align you with the rewards.

Besides, seeking the approval of man is like chasing leaves in the wind. You can never catch them all and the ones you do turn colors on you quickly. Seeking God's approval is all about reward! Not that we should be reward minded in what we do but just like Paul references in 1 Corinthians 9:24, every race has many runners but only one receives the prize and we should run to receive!

Our prize is eternity with God the Father and Christ our Savior. To gain that prize the race is long and hard and sometimes very lonely, but Christ carried His own cross, and hung on that cross alone for you and for me to have the opportunity to run for the prize.

In Hebrews 12 we are called to set our eyes on Jesus the one who shed His blood for us and suffered every form of humiliation on our behalf, yet He is now seated at the right hand of God. Hebrews 12:4 reminds us that we haven't yet resisted sin to the point of shedding blood. Wow, that is so powerful for me! When I think of things I have endured and many of them of my own making, I realize that nothing even slightly compares to the sacrifices Christ made for me and He was completely sinless and without blame.

What a wimpy little whiner I am! I suffer a little pain and I wonder if I can hold my ground. NO! I am in it to win it! You must be too! He is looking for worshipers who will worship Him in Spirit and in Truth! No compromise! Man will always have an opinion of what and who you are to be, but your Creator is the ONLY ONE that knows what and who you were MADE TO BE!

APPLICATION:

Can you think of a time when you stood up for your faith in an uncomfortable situation? If not, you may need to ask yourself why. If so, how did you feel? Were you nervous? Do you like or dislike confrontation? It can make a difference in how we handle many situations. Think about how you react and how you feel in situations where your faith is up for criticism or debate. Make some notes.

_____

_____

_____

_____

_____

Now, can you honestly say that the approval of God is more important in those moments than the approval of man? Our society gears us to stay away from the topic of faith. Look what happens to the people that talk openly and stand up for biblical principles and values; they are called haters! Well that is a lie straight from the pit of hell and if we don't tell the truth then we are allowing the enemies lie to perpetuate through us.

We have to make a choice, and you have to know what it is you believe in. Like the saying goes, "If you don't stand for something you will fall for anything."

Think about the people in your life that are the most difficult to talk to about spiritual things. Write their names down. Stop right now and pray for them. Pray that the Lord would open doors of opportunity to share with them and pray for them to have ears to hear. Pray for them daily and expect doors to open!

_____

_____

_____

_____

_____

Be bold and courageous, for we have not been given a spirit of fear!

🌳 STEP FOUR: Characteristics of Christ

We are called to be Christ-like, but if we don't know His nature it is impossible to be like Him. Let's look at a few that have been particularly important to me as I strive to be more like Him.

Humility is a very important part of who Christ is and how He presented Himself to the world when He walked among us. Paul explained in Philippines 2: 5-7 that Christ made himself of no reputation, taking on the form of a servant in the likeness of man. He didn't come looking for recognition for himself or to make himself grand in any way, He came proclaiming His Father in heaven.

How many times do we lose sight of what is really important while striving to have things or do things that have no eternal value? I see marriages and families ripped apart all the time by people who put their jobs and careers ahead of their families and their faith. There is no earthly gain that is greater than the purpose God has given you. Marriage, children, family and relationships are from God and should be cherished and nourished and seen as important work in the Kingdom. The titles we give ourselves are nothing more than that, just something to add to your signature line on stationary to tell the world and yourself that you are important. There is no one who you are more important to than your family.

Should we strive to be good at what we do? Absolutely! But our striving needs to be Honoring of our Father in heaven with all praise going to Him, knowing that without Him, we are nothing. It is humility in Spirit, understanding that our striving should be in the Fathers will for our life and He will direct us in His wisdom, therefore it is not of ourselves. Face to the floor, sold out, broken and humble before Him...that is our most powerful position.

APPLICATION:

What areas are taking up too much of your time and energy? What or who is getting more of your time than God? In what area does pride become an issue? Is it your job perhaps? That's pretty common. Remember that we are nothing without Christ so if you are striving for the bigger office, the better title and so forth, but you aren't home being the spiritual influence you should be then what have you gained? Humble yourself before the Lord and He will guide your path. Write those trouble areas down and commit them to the Lord daily.

_____

_____

_____

_____

Service is an important legacy that Christ left with us. He came in the form of a servant, not as a CEO, CFO, PHD or MD but as a servant. The disciple Matthew wrote a lot about the character of Christ. In Matthew 20:27, 28 He reminds us that Christ didn't come to be ministered to but to minister and to become a ransom for our sins. *'He came to minister not to be ministered to'.*

This verse struck me at a very important time in my life. I was walking with the Lord by then and was working hard to do the right things and I was in church every Sunday but I started to feel like I wasn't getting anything out of church anymore. It just seemed like people weren't as nice as I thought they should be and I saw petty arguments going on about the workings of the church and who was going to do what and so forth and I really began to think that I just wasn't going to attend anymore or I was going to find another church. I was praying about it one night and the Lord sent me to this verse. As I read the words … 'He came to minister not to be ministered to' … it hit me that I was attending church to be ministered to, but what was I doing to minister to others?

I think it is really easy to get focused on ourselves and not see all the opportunities around us to be used by God to minister to others. When we are focused on others we no longer have the time to dwell on ourselves and most of the time we will see how really good we have it in comparison to the needs of others. There is truly great joy in knowing you were able to help someone else.

My brokenness kept me in a state of wilderness living. Just like the Israelites I ran around the wilderness for 40 years (in my case it took a little longer ☹) grumbling and complaining and only seeing what I didn't have instead of seeing how truly blessed I was. When we are broken our energy is spent holding all the pieces together. It is a big job because we know how many pieces there are and we have to make sure that no one else figures it out! It was a hell of my own making because I believed every lie of the enemy. When we are focused on ourselves and on our own pain, our perception of everything around us is seen through that dark and ugly filter of 'self'.

Selfishness is often seen as egotism or self-promoting, but in reality selfishness is anytime you are focused on yourself. If you are beating yourself up for past mistakes, or whining because things are so difficult then there is no way you can see past yourself. You are in hell and it is called SELF! Look around! You want to feel better about your own situation? Just take a minute and invest in someone else and you will find that your situation isn't so bad, or at the very least, you are not alone! We all struggle, but we were made to serve one another. We were never made to do this thing called life by ourselves! Take your eyes off yourself, look at people with the eyes of Jesus and be amazed in how much you receive through a simple act of service. Don't seek to be served, but instead seek to serve others.

APPLICATION

Pray for the Lord to show you someone you can minister to through meeting a need. He will bring people to mind and make circumstances known to you if you are truly seeking those opportunities. Write down names as they come to you and pray over them.

_____

_____

_____

_____

Christ is Love! Love in the purest form. In John 15: 12, 13 Jesus tells us that there is no greater love than when someone is willing to lay down their life for someone else. It also says that we are to love each other the same way Christ loved us. Wait a minute…Jesus died for me. Yes that's right; we are to love each other with a love so great we would die for each other. Wow, that's a far cry from the excuses we find to not help out when called upon isn't it? The love of Christ is demonstrated through our service to one another. I love the expression that when we serve we are 'Jesus with skin on' because that's what people can see and touch and comprehend.

A loving and helping hand that is not looking for anything in return, only to serve and meet your needs in Jesus name. We are to love our neighbor, we are to love our enemies, and we are to love people as He loves them. Have you ever tried to love your enemy?

You can't do it if you are seeing them through the filter of self because then all you can see is how they can or have hurt you. Remember that hurting people hurt people, so when someone is hurting you they are hurting too. Ask God to help you see their hurt and how you can help, it causes a shift in the atmosphere and releases God's healing power over you both.

Love is not a feeling it is an action. You fall off things you don't fall in love. The warm, bubbly feeling that comes from being in love (pardon me I gagged a little) is of course exciting and wonderful and all of that but it is not what love IS. Love is putting someone else before yourself in a way that makes their happiness, provision and desires more important than your own.

Don't just tell people you love them; walk out that love in ways that show them how much you love them. Christ never said if you make money I will love you more. He never said if you look better I will love you more. He never said if you acquire more things and give me more things I will love you more... No, He not only said He loves us He opened His arms and showed us how much!

1 John 4:7-12 says that we are to love one another because love comes from God. So if we aren't showing real love to other people then we don't know God because God IS love.

That's pretty strong but that's what the bible says! When we show the love of the Father to one another then God's love can be completed in us! He lives in us, and His love is completed in us! I love that!

In my experience I have found that the people who are the most difficult to love are the ones who need it the most. I was one of those people and depending on who you talk to I might still be☺! Love is an act of obedience to the One who is love.

APPLICATION:

How do you show love? (If you bake cookies for people could you love me too please?☺) How do you receive love? What says "I love you' to you?
Who do you struggle to love? What makes it difficult?
Spend some time praying over the idea that love is an action not a feeling. Ask the Lord to show you how to take action in loving others.
Write down the names of those you struggle to love and pray for the Lord to show you those people

through His eyes. Pray to help you see past what is visible and see straight to the heart. Pray for the Lord to change your heart.

_____

_____

_____

_____

_____

_____

_____

_____

Websters
Love - 1 a (1) : strong affection for another arising out of kinship or personal ties <maternal love for a child> (2) : attraction based on sexual desire : affection and tenderness felt by lovers (3) : affection based on admiration, benevolence, or common interests <love for his old schoolmates> b : an assurance of love <give her my love>
2 : warm attachment, enthusiasm, or devotion

Bible
1 Corinthians 13:4 Love is patient, Love is kind. It does not envy, it does not boast, it is not proud. It is not rude, it is not self-seeking, it is not easily angered, it keeps no record of wrongs. Love does not delight in evil but rejoices with the truth. It always protects, always trusts, always hopes, always perseveres. Love never fails.
Vs. 13 And now these three remain: faith, hope and love, but the greatest of these is love.

See the difference? ☺

Obedience is an area that Christ once again set the ultimate example. Even while praying before He knew He was to be crucified in Matthew 26:39 He asked if He could get out if it and then in the same breath said even if He couldn't it was the Fathers will not His that He would carry out. Jesus wasn't all doped up on fairy dust running around with visions of lollipops in His head doing good and never suffering pain or ridicule for His actions. He suffered more than any of us could ever imagine but still remained obedient to His Father and the plan He had for Him.

It always amazes me when I hear people justify their sin with phrases like, "Well I know what the Bible says but God understands that I need to do this…" or "I know what the Bible says about it but this is a different time and that doesn't hold true anymore"…etc. etc. Well guess what, you don't know what the Bible says if you truly believe what you are saying! The Word of God is a living breathing road map to living beyond where we are and instead living in the full abundance of the Kingdom!

The Bible doesn't say…'oh you can skip this part if it doesn't suit you'…or 'this part is just for everyone living before the 1200's'. No! It says that He is the Alpha, the Omega, the beginning and the end and His Word is for the Ages! There isn't a single word of scripture that isn't relevant for today. The principles are the same yesterday today and tomorrow and it is up to you to choose if you are going to be obedient or not. Obedience is the key to living abundantly in the blessings of your benevolent Father.

Have you ever read what happens to a person that is crucified on a cross? It is the most painful, cruel and humiliating form of death that has ever been used in our society. Jesus is always seen as a mild and gentle man with His gentle blue eyes and often playing with the children. Yes well that is the Jesus I love and want to be around too, but the truth is, He was a mighty warrior and He suffered on the cross the most pain a human can suffer, and He did it in obedience to His father for no glory of His own.

He did it in obedience and He did it for you and for me. Is there really anything He asks from us that compares to that sacrifice? Is there anything the Father asks of us that compares to the sacrifice of killing your own child? Abraham understood the importance of obedience, and God honored his hearts desires more abundantly than Abraham could have ever imagined because Abraham put nothing before his faith and devotion to God. Gen 22: 16-18

APPLICATION:

What areas are you hanging on to? What scares you about total obedience? Write it down, commit it to prayer. The Lord changes us from the inside out and He sees our heart. As you commit it to prayer and faithfully seek to be obedient, your heart will begin to change. It is so important to write these things down. It is an acknowledgment even though you are the only one seeing it. Solutions start when problems are acknowledged.

_____

_____

_____

_____

_____

Forgiveness releases more power in our lives than anything else we can do.

Jesus understood the importance of forgiveness. Before going home and standing before His Father while hanging on the cross He asked His Father to 'forgive them, because they don't know what they are doing'. (Luke 23:24) You see Jesus gave us the perfect example of forgiveness because He was blameless yet He was hanging on the cross for crimes He didn't commit. At the same time He asked forgiveness for the people killing Him and He was dying for the guilty ones.

No greater act of forgiveness has ever been documented and it saved us all, but how many of us are practicing forgiveness in a way that honors His sacrifice? The popular quote by Louis B. Smedes says that "To forgive is to set a prisoner free and discover that the prisoner was you." I couldn't agree more!

Un-forgiveness traps us in a dark and selfish existence. It is like a cancer in our soul that eats away at anything good. We see the world through the eyes of pain, mistrust and anger. It begins to define who we are and how we present ourselves to the world. In Mark 11:25, 26 it is very clear that if we come before God for forgiveness and we are holding un-forgiveness in our heart toward someone else He cannot forgive us. If you are struggling to forgive someone look back at what we have learned; take your eyes off of yourself, ask the Lord to show you that person through His eyes, (remember hurting people hurt people) in humility commit to love them and to serve them, and once you do all that, the forgiveness will come.

I lived a life of hell because I was holding un-forgiveness against God, my parents and everyone else I could think of. That disease in my spirit was placed there by the lies of the enemy. If the enemy can keep us in a state of un-forgiveness he can keep us weak, and hateful and prickly.

The transformation won't happen right away but every time that person comes to mind go through the steps and it will happen. You are no longer looking at them through pain and anger, but now you are looking at them through the eyes of Christ which are eyes of compassion, grace and mercy. You have replaced the soul sucking cancer with rivers of living water and healing. Forgiveness is the key to freedom!

APPLICATION:

That's right! It is time to write down the people you struggle to forgive. If you fill up the lines move to the margins but you need to make sure not to miss anyone! This is an area you cannot take lightly. Your soul depends on it! Your joy and blessing rides on this! Be honest and thorough and as always, commit this to prayer!

_____
_____
_____
_____
_____
_____
_____

Divinely Supported! Jesus had the full support of His Father in everything He did. Guess what! You are also divinely supported! Jesus said that we would be able to do all that He had done and even greater because He knew where His power and strength came from and it is available to you too. All of the characteristics of Christ are within our grasp because we have the same power living in us! The power of the Holy Spirit dwells in us and gives us wisdom, strength and power.

We are never alone and we never have to rely on our own means, because as we walk out His purpose for our lives and as we seek to have the characteristics of Christ, the Father supports us and works all things together for our good. I referenced this verse earlier but Romans 8:28 is one of my favorite verses because it promises us that God is working ALL things together for good; it doesn't say just the things you've done right or well, it says ALL things. In a life full of broken pieces it is comforting to know that God holds all the pieces in His hands and He is shaping them in to a one of a kind masterpiece!

APPLICATION:

Take a second and think of all the things we have talked about and then write down the top three areas in which you know you need His strength. We need it in all things but there are those areas that we all have that are tougher than others because those areas are where we are the weakest. Before you can get them all written down, God is on His way to lift you up! Fall on your face and know that on your own you are nothing but with Him you can do ALL things!

_____

_____

_____

_____

There are many other characteristics we could look at like loyalty, kindness, bravery, and on and on but for us to understand where we need to be to change our lives from broken to beauty we need to understand these basics and strive to live them out. As we begin the transformation from brokenness to joyful and purposeful, we will take on His character more and more each day.

We are not called to be like other Christians, we are called to be like Christist. Author unknown

STEP FIVE: Praise Him in All Things

It is so easy to praise Him when things are going well but when life seems to fall apart around you and your circumstances look overwhelming, our praises are often silenced by grumbling and cries of desperation. Although He wants us to come to Him with our needs we can't forget to praise Him in the process.

I love the saying "When God closes a door, praise Him in the hallway!" because that tells the story of a heart for worship. The bottom line is that it doesn't matter what problems today may hold, God has always been there for me and He is there for me now! He knows my future and He has all the circumstances of my life under His control. He is working it all out for good! Remember? ☺

Praise is where His power is released in to the atmosphere. Have you ever been in a worship service and you feel the Spirit rising up within you and your hands are in the air or you feel tears beginning to form or you just stand motionless with a feeling of warmth pouring over you? The Spirit of the Lord and His power has been released in to the atmosphere.

It all goes back to the words we say. If we are praising God then we release His power in our circumstances, but if we are complaining and grumbling and all 'woe is me' then that is right where the enemy wants us so his power can be released, because he thrives on the fear, discontent, and doubt of God's people. That's his ticket into your heart and mind. He will worm his way in through the tiniest of openings so stay in praise. Slam that door shut on him and remind him that you are covered in the blood

of the lamb and no harm will come to you because
your daddy is the King!

When you need Jesus all you have to do is say the
name...Jesus and He comes running! When you
praise the name of Jesus, you will be able to feel the
wind in the atmosphere as the enemy flees! He will
flee faster than a rabbit on crack because he cannot
be in the presence of Jesus.

APPLICATION
Just take a few minutes and praise Him right now.
Whatever posture works for you but I encourage you
to physically come before the Lord and worship Him.
John 4:23 says that the Lord seeks worshipers that
will worship Him in Spirit and in Truth. Worship is
about honor, gratitude, obedience, love and sacrifice.
Seek Him, He is seeking you.

_____

_____

_____

_____

_____

_____

_____

STEP SIX: Tell your story!

One of the most important tools God uses is our own story. Your story is unique so tell it! We have each been brought to Jesus through different means and circumstances and He has changed us all in different ways and different times. My story may not be what resonates with someone in particular but your story might.

Nothing in our life has been by chance, we were all designed by God for a purpose and your story holds the key to that purpose. Even if you only tell it to one person when the Lord directs you to do so and that person comes to know the Lord, it was all worth it! My story is not one that will minister to everyone because not everyone can relate to what I have done and been through, but the Lord didn't tell me to save the world with my story, He told me to tell it and let Him decide who should hear it. I know that He is encouraging me to tell you to tell your story because He has people in mind that will benefit from your unique message.

He doesn't make idle requests, He doesn't make mistakes and He doesn't say things He doesn't mean. Obedience is an important Christ-like characteristic remember, so start thinking about your story, and tell it! It could be as simple as telling what the Lord did for you that day. When I was training corporately and the Lord provided safe travel for me that morning I would greet my class by saying, "praise God we are all here safely with the ability to learn!" or "thank you Lord for the great parking space" or whatever the case may be. Don't keep it to yourself, tell the world what the Lord is doing and has done for you. It makes a difference! If nothing else it opens the door to a conversation about faith. You never know who needs to have that conversation so take every opportunity to open the door for them to walk through.

There is healing for you in the telling of your story. I had lived 57 years and had been in ministry for many of those years and had led many people to Christ but I had never told my story to anyone. Bits and pieces of it here and there but never really told my story of rejection, abandonment, self-hatred, abuse and loss until the first RiseUp Women's Conference. I had a message all prepared and was ready to speak on the power of the tongue but God had another plan. He kept telling me I had to tell 'My Story'. Well…I kept telling Him that He was asking too much and that wasn't going to happen! Well He wouldn't leave me alone about it and the more I tried to prepare 'my' message the more it fell apart.

I can honestly tell you that I was trying to get out of it even after I was on stage and facing everyone! As it turned out, I was ministered to in a way I don't have words to explain, but I can tell you this, I was healed that day from the pain of my mistakes and chains broke off of me that I didn't even know were there. In telling my story I released the enemy's power over the pain that had held me captive. I didn't want anyone to know how really bad my life had been and the many horrible choices I had made and I believed the lies of the enemy that said I needed to hide it away.

Once I spoke it out loud, the enemy's power over that pain was gone and I was free to forgive myself and begin to live in the freedom Christ died to provide for me. I was told by women after women how that story resonated with them and how much they needed to hear it. They opened up to me about the pain they carried around and together we prayed for their freedom and we walk in that freedom together today.

So yes, the moral of the story is, be obedient and don't fight God...He really does know what's best for us!

APPLICATION

Start to write your story. Just snippets at this point but begin to think of what has made you who you are and write it down. As you have gone through this book you have started to identify a lot of what makes you who you are. Use that to tell your story.

_____

_____

_____

_____

_____

_____

_____

_____

_____

_____

_____

_____

STEP SEVEN: Speak Life! The number seven is the biblical number for completion, and I believe that there is no way to fully begin, persevere and complete your transformation until you learn to speak life! We will never be perfect but we can be transformed in to a person living in abundant blessing and joy. Real joy! Can you say you live in joy? I never even knew what that meant until it began to happen to me. I have always enjoyed making people laugh and have a good time but humor and laughter is different than joy. The Bible teaches that happiness is fleeting and temporary because it often depends on things outside of our self, but true joy is eternal because it is based on our relationship with Jesus Christ, which in itself is an eternal source of joy.

Depending on the translation the Bible uses the words 'happy' and 'happiness' about 30 times but the words 'joy' and 'rejoice' (which is where the word 'joy' comes from) appear over 300 times! That alone should tell you there is a difference and that joy should be the goal! Paul gave us a good picture of this in Philippians. Apostle Paul wrote this thank you letter to the believers of Philippi while imprisoned in Rome. The main theme of this letter is that only in Christ are real unity and joy possible. He uses the words 'joy', 'rejoice' and 'joyful' 16 times and teaches us about contentment despite our circumstances.

He is in chains and he knows his days are numbered but he still talks about his faith as reason to rejoice. He noted that all the Roman guard had heard the gospel during and because of his imprisonment. He counted it all joy! How many of us look at our circumstances and declare joy! The key to Paul's joy was in the Truth of what he knew in his heart to be true and his willingness to speak the truth even in situations that could get him killed. He understood the difference in a temporary feeling of happiness, which I am sure wasn't a common occurrence while in chains, and real joy which he proclaimed to everyone who could hear his voice. If he had been complaining or grumbling about his circumstances he wouldn't have been any different than anyone else in the prison.

Instead Paul understood that God's plan is perfect and way back when he made the decision to follow Christ he made the choice to trust Him and be obedient to the calling God had for him. He had joy knowing that everything was as it was meant to be and that God was fulfilling the purpose He had for Paul's life. Joy is a constant feeling of well-being that is not based on circumstances but instead on that knowledge that you belong to God, and He loves you and He has you in the palm of His hand. We have to believe these truths but we also have to speak the truth. The saving power of Jesus Christ is a message of Life! The story doesn't stop with His death; His death is only the beginning because He lives!

Speaking Life is so important to experiencing the joy Jesus died to give us. Speaking Life is about telling ourselves the Truth. Every word we say has an impact in the kingdom. We simply can't put too much importance on the words we speak. Look how important God feels our words are; He named His gift to us 'The Word'. He 'spoke' the world into existence. The Bible doesn't say he conjured up atoms and molecules and flung His arms and dramatically caused a great explosion or something it simply says for example, "He said, let there be light, and there was light." He said it, and it happened with the water, with man, with the animals, all of it! He spoke everything into being. That set the precedent for how the universe works. When we speak something into the atmosphere our words have power! If we are speaking the Truth then we are charging the atmosphere with God's power and Life! If however we are speaking the lies of the enemy (I am worthless, no one cares about me, my problems are worse than everyone else's, or you are stupid, I hate you, you will never learn, etc.) you are charging the atmosphere with the lies of the enemy and giving him power in your life and/or releasing the enemies power into the life you are speaking into.

Let's take a look at a really good example in Acts 16 where we find Paul and Silus teaching in the city and they came upon a slave-girl with the spirit of divination, and when Paul spoke to the spirit it left immediately. Paul didn't do a dance, he didn't beg or ask why she had the spirit he just spoke to it and told it to leave. Now the girls' masters were mad because now they aren't going to be able to profit from her so they came up with charges against Paul and Silus and had them imprisoned. Talk about no good deed goes unpunished! Here they are going about the work of the Lord and the next thing you know they are severely beaten, thrown in chains and dumped in a cold dark prison cell. What happens next is the key to the story; around midnight they began to <u>pray and sing praises to God</u> and the prisoners were listening! That one act of speaking life released God's power into the atmosphere and a great earthquake came and rattled the foundation until the doors stood open and the chains were broken off! The guard was so scared when he saw the doors open he was sure the prisoners had escaped and was going to kill himself. Paul spoke to him and said to not hurt himself because they were all there. The guard immediately asked what he had to do to be saved! Talk about signs and wonders! The guard knew that what happened in that moment was not of this world and it was more powerful than anything he had ever witnessed. The atmosphere was charged with the power of God because of the praise of His people. People imprisoned and in some of the darkest circumstances one can imagine; but they chose to praise Him and the atmosphere was changed!

They spoke the Truth to the guard and declared that to be saved he must believe in Jesus Christ as Savior. The guard took them to his home and there the Bible says that they 'spoke the word of the Lord' to him and to everyone in his house and that very night they were all saved and baptized. Paul and Silus changed the atmosphere of that home with the words of Truth and in doing so released the Spirit of the Lord to change their hearts and minds.

When it was all said and done Paul and Silus were also freed from the charges and were free to go about preaching and teaching. The outcome would have been very different if they had been moaning and crying in fear and anger for their circumstances. When we live in the joy of the Lord knowing that His plan is greater than our circumstances, miracles happen! What we say has to reflect that knowledge.

Speaking Life starts with our knowledge of Christ but it has to become a consciousness of the words we speak. I am the product of words of death being spoken over me every day of my life which then caused me to speak those words of death to myself and to others. Eventually words of death were all I could speak to myself and to others. Those words shaped my life and caused me to impact others in a negative way. Words change the atmosphere and therefore change outcomes.

We have to understand that the lesson of speaking life and death started in the Garden of Eden with a couple of trees. Yes that's right, trees. Remember the Tree of Life and the Tree of the Knowledge of Good and Evil? Well, there was a good reason that God didn't want Adam and Eve eating from that tree and it has nothing to do with apples. It was about living in life and not death. You see Adam and Eve were in paradise. The Word says that they could hear God walking in the garden. Wouldn't that be awesome to be so close to God to hear His movements?! They lacked for nothing. They had been provided with everything they needed. They were naked but it didn't bother them, they were living as God had created them to be... free! Well Satan couldn't let them worship God so he had to introduce that thing called sin.

When the conversation took place between Eve and the serpent (the enemy) it was clear that Eve knew she was not to eat from the Tree of the Knowledge of Good and Evil and she understood the consequences; if she did she would die. That is what the enemy used to win her over, he mocked the belief that she would die and instead told her she would be like God knowing good and evil. There you have it, when Eve fell death entered the garden. A key word in all this is the 'knowledge' of good and evil. For example, they weren't concerned about their nakedness until sin entered into the equation. Now instead of living freely in paradise and communion with God, they began to find fault, and the knowledge of sin began to change how they spoke. When God asked them if they ate from the tree Adam's response was that the 'woman God gave him' had given it to him, so he was blaming Eve and God! Then Eve blamed the serpent and said he had deceived her even though she had full understanding of her disobedience and the consequences.

Blame, guilt, fear, shame, disobedience and pain have now entered the kingdom and would be used from that moment on by the enemy to control and weaken God's people. The enemy has one goal, and that is to take as many of God's people with him as he can when he is finally cast into the lake of fire. The knowledge of good and evil is the toolbox of the enemy.

If you are finding fault with yourself, then you are right where the enemy wants you. When you are believing His lies that you are not enough, you are worthless, you need to be more, be different, do more, do less, if you only hadn't done that, or if you had only done things differently, and on and on, it is just like that moment when Adam and Eve realized they were naked...you are ashamed and hiding from the Lord. If you are finding fault in other people and speaking death into their life, you are being used by the enemy to bring them to the same point of shame, guilt and worthlessness before God.

The Word says the tongue is a two edged sword. If you are swinging that ugly sword at someone else you leave them bloody and weak but the same is true when you are swinging that sword at yourself. With every blow of that sharp edge you are bleeding and weakened. Galatians 5 tells us that we are to love our neighbor as ourselves. Well if we hate ourselves that hatred has nowhere to go but out and flow on to everyone else and it comes out through our words.

The enemy persuaded Eve with his lying words and that is how he works in and through us, with his lies. We have to speak against the lies of the enemy. I was told I was stupid and ugly and worthless every day in the halls of school until I believed it. I must be stupid, I know I'm ugly because I am fat and I don't have pretty store bought clothes and fancy dresses. I must stink because they say I do. I must be an awful person because they say I am. Remember, I'm so ugly my parents died of embarrassment. It is impossible to hear those things and not be impacted by them. The words we speak have the power of life and death and I knew all about death. The words spoken over me started me on the road to self-destruction because I believed I was worthless and too ugly to live so I longed for death to end my pain.

When someone finally came along and spoke truth to me and understood that I didn't know how to receive words of life, and they helped me to start thinking differently, that's when I started to live!

APPLICATION

This time I want you to pray first and ask God to show you the words of life you need to hear. If there are areas of your life that you are not speaking truth about, He will reveal those areas to you. Just be still and listen as He begins to speak words of truth to your heart and ask Him to show you the lies you are carrying. As He begins to reveal those to you write them down. Look at them and ask the Lord to help you change your mind and heart about the messages you are hearing.

If you are hearing messages that are making you feel inadequate or unworthy then tell that voice to shut up and send it packing because that is the enemy, that is not God!

_____

_____

_____

_____

_____

_____

_____

_____

_____

THE TRUTH WILL SET YOU FREE

Have you ever heard that phrase? I am sure you have. What does it mean to you? Well, I know from living a life of lies that it means far more than always telling the truth to your friends and family, and if you cut down a cherry tree to be honest about it! ☺

The enemy is the Prince of Lies! His whole reign and existence is based on the lie that the Truth is not the Truth and you are not who you were made to be. Until you understand that you are fearfully and wonderfully made for a specific purpose in the Kingdom of Heaven, and you begin to grasp the power that you have been given by your birthright, you will never fully live in the freedom that Truth provides in abundance!

What is truth? Ephesians says in Chapter 1 that once we have heard the word of truth, you will trust it and believe it and when that happens we are then 'sealed' with the Holy Spirit of promise! Promise! We are so used to people promising things and then not delivering on those promises that when we hear of the 'promises of God' or the 'Holy Spirit of promise', it doesn't seem to move us much. The first step in understanding and truly believing in Truth is to never compare it to anything we know or currently understand. People will always fail us but God is incapable of failure!

We need to get a grasp on the fact that God always fulfills His promises! He is not capable of deceit, He is Truth! The only hope we have for our future that can absolutely be counted on is the Truth of the Word of God! His promises have to be fulfilled because He cannot and will not fail!

THE MOSAIC

I can't even begin to tell you all the things I have had to forgive myself for. I can tell you this; there is not one commandment I left unbroken. Yes, that includes murder. I had an abortion when my daughter was still a toddler. I was overwhelmed and high most of the time and I was barely getting by so I couldn't imagine having another child. I wasn't a good mother to the child I already had. Even with all that said, I have tears running down my face as I type this because I still don't know who that woman was that gave up her beautiful child to an abortion. Of all the things I have brought before the Lord and asked forgiveness for that's the one thing I still struggle with. I know He has forgiven me; I am still working on forgiving myself.

You may have things in your life that you just don't think anyone would understand, and you keep them buried deep, but I am here to tell you that is a death sentence! There is freedom in sharing your story and there is healing in laying it before God. Don't believe the lies of the enemy! You are not the choices you've made, you are a masterpiece in the Hands of your Creator and He has a purpose for you!

I have been married and divorced, I have committed adultery, I have been raped twice, I have been beaten more times than I can count, I have done drugs, lied, stole, cheated and all the rest, but that is not who I am. I have gone through the fire of refinement and have come through changed. The word refinement means the process of removing impurities or unwanted elements from a substance. When we choose the path of righteousness He refines us. He speaks life in to us and takes the brokenness and removes the sharp edges and molds us in to a completely new and refined creature.

The choices I made and the things I did have given me compassion and a heart for the lost that I wouldn't have had otherwise. I have insight in to broken lives that others wouldn't see. God is taking all the broken pieces and making them valuable for His purpose and the work of His Kingdom.

Come join me and kick off the last bit of the cocoon; it's time for God's beautiful creatures to fly!

43 But now thus saith the LORD that created thee, O Jacob, and he that formed thee, O Israel, Fear not: for I have redeemed thee, I have called thee by thy name; thou art mine.

2 When thou passest through the waters, I will be with thee; and through the rivers, they shall not overflow thee: when thou walkest through the fire, thou shalt not be burned; neither shall the flame kindle upon thee.

3 For I am the LORD thy God, the Holy One of Israel, thy Saviour:

King James Version (KJV)

www.ingramcontent.com/pod-product-compliance
Lightning Source LLC
Chambersburg PA
CBHW062024040426
42447CB00010B/2124